A LIFEBUILDER  BIBLE STUDY

NEW TESTAMENT CHARACTERS

*12 Studies
for individuals or groups*

Carolyn Nystrom

With Notes for Leaders

SCRIPTURE UNION
130 City Road, London EC1V 2NJ

First published in the United States by InterVarsity Press
First published in Great Britain by Scripture Union, 1993
Reprinted 1995

ISBN 0 86201 894 3

Cover photograph: Peter French

Printed in England by Ebenezer Baylis & Son Limited, The Trinity Press, Worcester, and London

Contents

Contents

Getting the Most
from LifeBuilder Bible Studies

Many of us long to fill our minds and our lives with Scripture. We desire to be transformed by its message. LifeBuilder Bible Studies are designed to be an exciting and challenging way to do just that. They help us to be guided by God's Word in every area of life.

How They Work

LifeBuilders have a number of distinctive features. Perhaps the most important is that they are *inductive* rather than *deductive*. In other words, they lead us to *discover* what the Bible says rather than simply *telling* us what it says.

They are also thought-provoking. They help us to think about the meaning of the passage so that we can truly understand what the author is saying. The questions require more than one-word answers.

The studies are personal. Questions expose us to the promises, assurances, exhortations and challenges of God's Word. They are designed to allow the Scriptures to renew our minds so that we can be transformed by the Spirit of God. This is the ultimate goal of all Bible study.

The studies are versatile. They are designed for student, neighborhood and church groups. They are also effective for individual study.

How They're Put Together

LifeBuilders also have a distinctive format. Each study need take no more than forty-five minutes in a group setting or thirty minutes in personal study – unless you choose to take more time.

The studies can be used within a quarter system in a church and fit well in a semester or trimester system on a college campus. If a guide has more than thirteen studies, it is divided into two or occasionally three parts of approximately twelve studies each.

LifeBuilders use a workbook format. Space is provided for writing answers to each question. This is ideal for personal study and allows group members to prepare in advance for the discussion.

The studies also contain leader's notes. They show how to lead a group discussion, provide additional background information on certain questions, give helpful tips on group dynamics and suggest ways to deal with problems which may arise during the discussion. With such helps, someone with little or no experience can lead an effective study.

Suggestions for Individual Study

1. As you begin each study, pray that God will help you to understand and apply the passage to your life.

2. Read and reread the assigned Bible passage to familiarize yourself with what the author is saying. In the case of book studies, you may want to read through the entire book prior to the first study. This will give you a helpful overview of its contents.

3. A good modern translation of the Bible, rather than the King James Version or a paraphrase, will give you the most help. The New International Version, the New American Standard Bible and the Revised Standard Version are all recommended. However, the questions in this guide are based on the New International Version.

4. Write your answers in the space provided in the study guide. This will help you to express your understanding of the passage clearly.

5. It might be good to have a Bible dictionary handy. Use it to look up any unfamiliar words, names or places.

Suggestions for Group Study

1. Come to the study prepared. Follow the suggestions for individual study mentioned above. You will find that careful preparation will greatly enrich your time spent in group discussion.

2. Be willing to participate in the discussion. The leader of your group will not be lecturing. Instead, he or she will be encouraging the members of the group to discuss what they have learned from the passage. The leader will be asking the questions that are found in this guide. Plan to share what God has taught you in your individual study.

3. Stick to the passage being studied. Your answers should be based on the verses which are the focus of the discussion and not on outside authorities such as commentaries or speakers. This guide deliberately avoids jumping from book to book or passage to passage. Each study focuses on only one

passage. Book studies are generally designed to lead you through the book in the order in which it was written. This will help you follow the author's argument.

4. Be sensitive to the other members of the group. Listen attentively when they share what they have learned. You may be surprised by their insights! Link what you say to the comments of others so the group stays on the topic. Also, be affirming whenever you can. This will encourage some of the more hesitant members of the group to participate.

5. Be careful not to dominate the discussion. We are sometimes so eager to share what we have learned that we leave too little opportunity for others to respond. By all means participate! But allow others to also.

6. Expect God to teach you through the passage being discussed and through the other members of the group. Pray that you will have an enjoyable and profitable time together.

7. If you are the discussion leader, you will find additional suggestions and helpful ideas for each study in the leader's notes. These are found at the back of the guide.

Introducing New Testament Characters

Most of us see ourselves as little people: minor characters. We travel within a few hundred miles. We live within a few dozen years. We touch a few hundred lives. In the big scene, the whole sweep of history and geography, we matter little. But that does not make us unimportant. Something inside us shouts against that smallness. We know that we matter: to our friends, to our families, to ourselves. And we matter to God.

As if to reinforce our view of our own importance, the New Testament is full of little people. Sure, we can trace major characters through chapter after chapter: Peter, Paul, James, John and, of course, Jesus. Their names and activities charted the course of Christendom. But surrounding these major characters are ordinary people: Thomas, one of Christ's lesser disciples whose questions and doubts led him to faith; Philemon, who had to decide what to do with a dishonest slave who ran away and then got religion; Priscilla and Aquila, who opened their home to traveling missionaries and eventually to a whole church; a nameless prison guard in Philippi who gave the apostle Paul a beating, then said yes to God in a single night; Governor Felix, who toyed with the gospel for two years—and then said no.

Ordinary people, each meriting a few paragraphs of Scripture. But we see ourselves in these people. And as we trace their impact, we also see that we, too, make a difference. Who we are and what we do is important. We are ordinary people, but we matter to God.

1
Joseph: Parenting in Tough Times
Matthew 1:18-25; 2:13-23

Do you sometimes feel that today's family is in decline? Television comedies picture weak parents with mouthy (but oh so clever) children. Newspapers shout threats of murder, rape and drugs. Support groups form almost overnight for single parents, families of alcoholics, and survivors of family abuse. And these can hardly keep up with the need.

But even in the more simple era of two thousand years ago, Joseph's job as parent was no simple task. Joseph lived in an occupied land where political enemies did not target their hostilities at adults alone. Joseph had to move his family long distances—quickly and on short notice. And then there were the angels . . .

1. What do you think is difficult about being a father today?

2. Read Matthew 1:18-25. What unusual circumstances did Joseph face during his engagement and early marriage?

3. What alternatives to his planned marriage do you think that he considered?

4. Verse 19 says that Joseph was a righteous man. How do you think Joseph's righteousness contributed to the way he handled the events here?

5. What information did God reveal to Joseph?

How might this information help Joseph in his work as husband and father?

6. Study the names given to the new baby. What do they reveal about the importance of Joseph's job?

7. Read Matthew 2:13-23. What new responsibilities faced Joseph at this point?

8. If you had been the father of this young family, what would you be worrying about during these events?

9. We have read of three instances in which an angel of the Lord spoke to Joseph. What would it be like to have angels speak to you in this way?

How do you think these experiences affected Joseph?

10. God used a human family to care for and protect the infant Jesus. Have you felt protected emotionally or physically within your own family? Explain.

11. We experience both love and pain in any family. Some families draw us to God by their example of faith. Others drive us to God by the emptiness they create. How has God used your family to nudge you toward spiritual maturity?

2
Anna and Simeon: Growing Old with God
Luke 2:21-40

I wonder what Sheri will be like when she is old," mused my prospective son-in-law. "I can't wait to see her then—all wrinkles, but just as much laughter as ever."

It seemed an odd comment from a twenty-two-year-old with decades of life ahead of him. But Joel planned a marriage that would last, and lasting power meant old age. "I want us to grow old together," he said.

Perhaps more of us will enter old age with greater grace if we plan for it before we get there.

---

1. What do you want to be like when you are old?

---

2. Read Luke 2:21-35. Why did Jesus and his family go to Jerusalem?

---

3. In what ways was Simeon already prepared to meet Jesus (vv. 25-27)?

4. What did Simeon know about the past—and the future (vv. 29-35)?

5. Simeon's prayer is the Nunc Dimittis, a Latin term meaning "now dismiss." Why did Simeon feel that he was ready for God to dismiss him from this life in peace?

6. What would you like to happen so that you could say at the end of your life, "Lord, now dismiss your servant in peace"?

7. Read Luke 2:36-40. Why might you say that Anna's life was difficult, but fulfilling?

8. How did God use Anna?

9. How did the next stage of Christ's life prepare him to do and be what Anna and Simeon had predicted (vv. 39-40)?

10. What do you admire about the aging characters in this story?

11. What could you do now to prepare for an old age that is at peace with God?

3
A Throw-away Woman: Redeemed by Christ

John 8:1-11

My friend "Tom" is a throw-away person. Not to me and not to God. But to most people, Tom is a nuisance, best jollied out of a foul mood or ignored like a pesky child. But Tom is a real man.

Plagued by mental illness, he has lost his home, his marriage, his church, and over seventy jobs. (Imagine the effort it took to *find* seventy jobs!) Sometimes Tom can barely get out of bed. At other times, he can't sleep—for night after night. Some days his mind flits at fast forward with no pause button for organization. On other days his mind plods so slowly that he can't figure out a sales slip. Tom is nobody's favorite dinner guest.

Some people are kind to Tom—though few admit him to friendship. Others simply use him: as low-paid worker, as the butt of a joke. To them, Tom is like Kleenex, used once and thrown in the trash.

Yet Tom is real. His laughter is real, and so are his tears. But he joins a host of others who can't quite function in today's society. If society were an assembly line, people like Tom would land in the discard heap.

---

1. What kinds of people does our society tend to "throw-away"?

---

2. Read John 8:1-6a. What events lead to Christ's meeting with the woman?

3. What evidence do you see that the temple leaders were using this woman for their own purposes?

No name, brought woman, etc.

---

4. When have you sensed that you were being treated like trash?

What effect did that experience have on you?

---

5. Leviticus 20:10, "If a man commits adultery with another man's wife—with the wife of his neighbor—both the adulterer and the adulteress must be put to death," is the law that these religious leaders had in mind. In view of that law, why do you think that they brought the woman—but not the man?

A trap for woman. Freer men?

Woman less important

---

6. Verse 6 refers to a trap. Why was their question a trap? (See also John 18:31.)

Jesus caught both law — death. Roman law — denied enforcement — whatever he did guilty × one place.

---

7. What underlying problems were not being addressed by the accusations against the woman?

Christs Authority. Forgiveness. John 9 womens life

---

8. Read John 8:6b-11. How did Christ's actions show that the woman was not a throw-away person in his sight?

Did he erase her actions.

9. Jesus spoke to both the woman and the religious leaders about sin. Why?

10. Jesus showed that he valued the woman even though the temple leaders did not. What words or actions help you to feel valued?

11. What difference does it make to you that Christ values you—no matter what you have done?

12. The religious leaders used the woman to gain what they thought was a greater good. What is wrong with using people in this way?

13. Many people are almost faceless to us. We see them only for what they can do for us. With other people we avoid them because their problems are too big for us to fix, or because they embarrass us. Think of some of the "throw-away people" who enter your life. How might you treat these people in a way that mirrors Christ?

4
A Blind Beggar: Seeing Jesus with Open Eyes
John 9

Open our eyes, Lord. We want to see Jesus.
To reach out and touch him, and say that we love him.
Open our ears, Lord, and help us to listen.
Open our eyes, Lord. We want to see Jesus.
BOB CULL

We want to see Jesus, hear him, know him. But sometimes we feel almost blind and deaf and unfeeling to his touch. Yet, if we review our history with Jesus, we will find times when he has indeed opened our eyes. And bit by bit he has grown our faith.

This was also true of a first-century blind man, blind both physically and spiritually. But Jesus opened his eyes. And slowly, step by faltering step, the blind man "saw" Jesus.

1. What are some of your earliest mental pictures of Jesus?

2. Read John 9. What do you admire about the blind man?

3. What do you think Christ's words in verses 1-5 meant to the blind man at this point?

4. How would you describe the beggar's faith as he responded to the situations in verses 6-12?

5. Study the beggar's conversation with the Pharisees in verses 13-34. What pressures did he have to cope with?

6. Notice the references to sin in verses 1-2, 29 and 34. Why are these kinds of accusations particularly painful?

What is wrong with the view of sin portrayed by these accusations?

7. Verse 16 says that the Pharisees were divided in their opinion of Jesus. Why?

How did the beggar draw on the debate he had heard between the Pharisees as he developed his own view of Jesus?

8. Study Christ's closing conversation with the beggar in verses 35-41. How did the events leading to verse 34 prepare the beggar for this second meeting with Jesus?

---

9. Study the beggar's statements of faith in verses 11-12, 17, 25, 27, 30-33, and 36-38. How does each statement reflect a gradual opening of his spiritual eyes?

---

10. What are some of the stages that your own faith has passed through?

---

11. If you were to explain to the Pharisees Christ's statement about blindness and sight in verses 39-41, what would you say to them?

---

12. The beggar spent many years in darkness preparing to see. How have the "dark times" of your own life prepared you for deeper faith in Jesus?

5
Lazarus: A Man Who Died Twice
John 11:1-44

In the spring, crocuses bloom on my daughter's grave. It's the fourth spring now, nearly four years since a car wreck took her life and the life of her unborn child. That first fall, just weeks after her death, I dug dried bulbs into the ground, willing myself to believe that by spring they'd blossom and convince me of life within their earth-bound cage. Each fall, I've added more bulbs, a garden of hyacinths, scilla, daffodils, snowdrops, red tulips (her favorite color). And each spring, I pick around in the grass, finding the first shoots that reassure me of resurrection—theirs and hers.

The early numbness that had me standing over her wrecked car and sobbing, "No, it's not her. It can't be," has been replaced. And I have had to know that Sheri is indeed gone from this life. Yet somewhere inside, even after all these years, I resist that fact. Just this week, I dreamed that Sheri was alive and well and talking with me—planning for her future. Death is hard to accept.

1. Why is the reality of death so hard for us to grasp?

2. Read John 11:1-16. What does this passage tell you about the relationship between Mary, Martha, Lazarus and Jesus?

3. If you had been one of Christ's disciples, what would you be saying and thinking on your walk south to Bethany?

4. How might Christ's words soften the disciples' fears about the trip?

5. Read John 11:17-37. What signs of a home in grief do you see in this section?

6. If you have experienced the death of someone near you, what kinds of help did you particularly appreciate at that time?

7. Study Christ's conversation with his friend Martha in verses 21-27. What comfort could Martha find in Christ's words of verse 25?

8. What all did Martha include in her personal statement of faith (vv. 24, 27)?

9. What comfort did Jesus offer to his friend Mary (vv. 33-37)?

10. Look again at the accusations in verses 21, 32 and 37. What did these people know and not know about Jesus?

11. Read John 11:38-44. If you had been in the crowd outside the tomb, what thoughts and feelings would you have had?

What questions would remain in your mind?

12. If you were Lazarus, do you think you would want to be raised from the dead? Explain.

13. Although we can't raise the dead, what are some ways we can follow Jesus' example and comfort those in grief?

6
Mary Magdalene: Loving Jesus in Practical Ways
Luke 8:1-3; Mark 15:37-47; John 20:1-18

Twelve men followed Jesus. He chose these disciples early, while his ministry still centered in Galilee; all but one of them came from that region where Christ himself grew up. These men followed Jesus for three years, listened to his teachings, assisted in his acts of kindness. So special was their role in Christ's ministry that later writers called them "The Twelve."

But Jesus had other followers too. The women. Some are nameless. Others appear with their sons' names. And some walk through the pages of text with their own names intact. These women also assisted in Christ's work. They too learned from his teachings. And they served Jesus in practical ways that some of the men seemed to forget. Mary Magdalene was one of these.

1. What are some practical ways that you have seen people express love?

2. Read Luke 8:1-3. What can you know about Mary Magdalene from these verses? (Consider her past, her work, her friends.)

3. Read Mark 15:37-47. Why do you think Mary Magdalene chose to be present at Christ's death?

4. What would she have seen and heard and learned and felt as she watched Christ die?

5. What changes had to take place in Mary Magdalene for her to move from a person inhabited by seven demons to the person who followed Jesus all the way to his death?

6. Jesus delivered Mary Magdalene from seven demons. What influences of evil has Jesus defeated in your own life?

7. Read John 20:1-18. If you were a detective observing all the events in these verses, what "clues" would you record?

8. What variety of feelings do you sense in the meeting between Mary Magdalene and Jesus?

9. Study Christ's statement in verse 17. What does it reveal about the relationships between the various people mentioned?

10. What effect would Mary Magdalene's message have on the disciples—and on the future church?

11. Meditate for a moment on the ways Christ's death and resurrection have influenced your own life. How are you different because of the events Mary Magdalene witnessed on those days?

12. Briefly skim all three passages. What all do you find that shows Mary Magdalene as a person who exercised her love for Jesus in practical ways?

13. What are some practical ways that you can show your own love for Jesus?

7
Thomas: Disciple of Doubt
John 14:1-7; 20:19-31

It descended one day like a dark cloud. The niggling questions that had pricked at the back of my mind for months suddenly clumped into one large doubt. Maybe Jesus didn't really rise from the dead. Maybe it was all a skillful hoax. Maybe I, along with other deluded Christians, was one whom the apostle Paul had described as "to be pitied more than all men."

I prayed. I read the Scriptures. I talked with believing friends. I read commentaries about the resurrection. Still I doubted. One respected friend laughed her own form of disbelief—at me. "No Christian of three decades' standing could seriously ask such questions," she said. Did she think I was playing some school-girl game?

In the end, the doubts settled. And my faith strengthened—even more than before.

---

1. What would you say or do if you had a close friend who was encountering serious doubts about the Christian faith?

2. Christ's followers had been with him for three years. Though they didn't know it, his death was a mere day away. John 14 begins Christ's last major recorded conversation with his disciples. Read John 14:1-7. What all could the disciples know, from these words, about Christ's future and their own (vv. 1-4)?

3. What value did Thomas's question have for himself and the others who heard Christ's words (vv. 5-7)?

4. What difference does it make that Jesus said, "I *am* the way, the truth, and the life," instead of "I *know*" or "I *taught you* the way, the truth, and the life"?

5. What words here comfort you? Explain.

6. Jesus died (as he said he would) and was buried on Friday. John 20 records what happened on Sunday. Read John 20:19-31. What all did Thomas miss by not being present with the rest of the disciples on Sunday night (vv. 19-23)?

7. In view of the differences between what the ten disciples had experienced and what Thomas had experienced, how do you think Thomas and the ten differed in the way they spent their next week?

8. How did Jesus deal with Thomas's doubts (vv. 26-29)?

_____

9. What internal changes had to take place for Thomas to say the words of verse 28?

_____

10. What is your own place in the picture described in verses 29-31?

_____

11. How might a period of doubt, such as Thomas experienced, have a long-term positive effect?

_____

12. John 20:31 says that "by believing you may have life in his name." How has belief in Christ's death and resurrection given you life?

8
Simon: Bargaining with God

Acts 8:9-25

"There are no atheists in foxholes," wrote William T. Cummings in 1942 in his *Sermons on Bataan*. While crouched in a trench with bullets zinging overhead, even the most reluctant heart begins to bargain with God—just in case he might exist. "God, if you'll only get me out of this alive, I'll . . ." But foxhole faith rarely lasts. The crisis passes, and thoughts of God recede to the background. To the foxhole "Christian" God is there mostly for emergencies.

But foxholes are not the only bargaining fields with God. Too many of us relate to God mostly for what we think we can gain from that relationship. In ancient Samaria, a man named Simon stands as an example of all that is wrong with attempts to use God for our own designs.

1. Why do people try to bargain with God?

2. Read Acts 8:9-17. What words here reveal the kind of man Simon was (vv. 9-13)?

3. What danger was Simon to the people who followed him?

4. What indications do you see that Simon's practice of sorcery would not fit with his new faith in Jesus?

5. Why did Peter and John go from Jerusalem to Samaria (vv. 14-17)?

6. Read Acts 8:18-25. What precisely did Simon want, and how did he propose to get it (vv. 18-19)?

7. What uses might Simon have planned to make of this gift?

8. What did Simon's offer suggest that he believed about God?

about the abilities God gives to his people?

9. What all, according to Peter, was wrong with Simon's attitude and his offer (vv. 20-23)?

10. Study Simon's response in verse 24. Do you think this represented genuine repentance or another attempt to bargain with God? Explain.

---

11. What, other than money, do people use to try to get what they want from God?

---

12. Take a moment to name a dozen or so of God's attributes. For example, "God is holy, God is kind, God has all power," and so on.

How might you adjust your praying so that it better reflects what you know to be true of God, rather than what you hope to get from him?

9
A Prison Guard: Getting Free from Internal Prisons
Acts 16:6-40

In the first century, in what is now the country of Bulgaria, lay the city of Philippi. It was ten miles inland from the Aegean Sea, on a plain between two rivers with gold-rich Mount Pangaeus to the west. The city straddled a major trade route, the Via Egnatia, which headed for the seaport Neapolis.

Philippi had earned its name in 356 B.C. from ruler Philip II, who named it, of course, for himself. But in 167 B.C. the city became a Roman colony. By the time of Christ's birth, Philippi was home to many retired Roman Army veterans who had fought on the wrong side of internal political wars. It also housed a famous medical school, the probable alma mater of Luke, author of the book of Acts.

Like many ethnocentric Roman communities, Philippi had little tolerance for "odd" faiths and practices. The ruins of an arch one mile west of town still stand as reminder of that intolerance. Outside that gate lay cemeteries, meeting sites of foreign religions, and all else that Romans classified as "impure." The River Gangites flows nearby, a likely spot where the apostle Paul met a woman named Lydia.

The city of Philippi was not a friendly place to start a church. But Paul did just that.[1]

---

1. What attracts you to your particular church congregation?

2. Read Acts 16:6-15. How did the Christian church in Philippi begin?

3. What does this passage tell you about Lydia's character that would make her a capable founding member of that church?

4. Read Acts 16:16-40. Since the slave girl was telling the truth about God, why do you think that Paul told the evil spirit to leave her (vv. 16-19)?

5. What evil influences complicate your own life?

6. Christ's power is greater than any power of evil—which is why Paul could command the evil spirit to leave the girl in the name of Jesus Christ. As you reflect on the power of Jesus, what practical steps can you take in your struggle against the evil that touches your own life?

7. Look again at verses 19-21. What problems for the new church in Philippi were the charges against Paul and Silas likely to create?

8. The prison guard was himself a prisoner: a prisoner to his job, and a prisoner to his inner fears. What all did God do to free him from each of those prisons?

9. Paul told the jailer, "Believe in the Lord Jesus, and you will be saved—you and your household." What freedoms does this new relationship with Jesus provide?

_____

10. If Jesus is your Lord, what structure does this bring to your life?

_____

11. From what you can see of the jailer's actions, why do you think that he would be a valuable addition to the new Christian church in Philippi?

_____

12. How did Paul's method of leaving Philippi act as further protection for the church he had founded (vv. 37-40)?

_____

13. When you think of the future of your church, what worries come to your mind?

What can you do to help protect your church from the kind of harm that you envision?

[1] Arthur Rupprecht in _The Zondervan Pictorial Encyclopedia of the Bible,_ ed. Merrill C. Tenney (Grand Rapids, Mich.: Zondervan, 1975), 4:759-62.

10
Priscilla and Aquila: Practicing Hospitality

Acts 18

She makes you feel when you arrive
How good it is to be alive.
She promptly orders fresh-made tea
However late the hour may be.
She leads you to a comfy room
With fire ablaze—and flowers abloom.
She shows you cupboards large and wide,
No hats or frocks of hers inside!
A writing-table meets your eye,
The newest novels on it lie.
The bed is just a nest of down,
Her maid puts out your dinner-gown.
The water's hot from morn 'til night,
Her dinners fill you with delight.
She never makes you stand for hours
Admiring children, dogs or flowers!
What better way to please her guest?
The Perfect Hostess lets you rest.
ELIZABETH PAGET, in *The Perfect Hostess*
compiled by Rose Henniker Heaton, 1931

We smile at this genteel expression of hospitality from a past generation. Today's fast-paced host or hostess may order pizza and rent a movie—and please the guest just as well. But, though the preparations differ, the warm feeling of hospitality doesn't change. Hospitality was a gift even in the apostle Paul's era. And he was the recipient.

1. What do you do to prepare for houseguests?

When you are a guest, what forms of hospitality do you most enjoy?

2. Read Acts 18 and Romans 16:3-5a. In what different ways did Priscilla and Aquila show hospitality?

3. Focus on Acts 18. Why would Paul be a difficult houseguest?

4. What local controversies do you think Paul discussed with Priscilla and Aquila around the kitchen table at night (Acts 18:1-17)?

5. What evidence do you see that, in spite of the hostile atmosphere, God was using Paul in Corinth (Acts 18:8-11)?

6. What do you think Priscilla and Aquila's hospitality contributed to Paul's ability to do God's work in Corinth?

7. What do you think Priscilla and Aquila gained from Paul?

8. When have you grown spiritually or emotionally because of the presence of a guest in your home?

9. What further examples of hospitality do you see among the early Christians in this text (Acts 18:18-28)?

10. Why do you think Priscilla and Aquila traveled with Paul as far as Ephesus—then stayed there (Acts 18:24-28)?

11. What reasons did Apollos have to be grateful to Priscilla and Aquila?

12. Look again at Romans 16:3-5a. What would be difficult about having a church meet in your home?

What would be rewarding?

13. What are some practical ways that you can use your own home (or room, or phone) to accomplish God's work?

11
Governor Felix: Saying "Wait" to God

Acts 24

The apostle Paul and the Roman Governor Felix marched toward each other on a collision course. Paul had returned to Jerusalem from his third missionary trip. In an attempt to mend relationships with the Jews, he worshiped in the temple, being careful to observe the most strict religious purification laws. But Jews, who knew that Paul had spent the last decade teaching Gentiles about the new Christian faith, incited a riot. Roman soldiers eventually rescued Paul by protecting him in their own barracks. When forty Jews plotted to neither eat nor drink until Paul was dead, the Roman commander took four hundred and seventy troops and escorted Paul by night sixty miles north to Caesarea for safe-keeping—and for trial.

Felix, governor of Caesarea, had moved from slavery, to freedom, to high government power. He married at least three times. His third wife, Drusilla, was a mere girl who had married the King of Emesa at fifteen, but whom Felix seduced for himself a year later. Historian Tacitus described Felix as "a master of cruelty and lust who held the power of a tyrant with the disposition of a slave." He would decide Paul's fate.

1. When do you have trouble making decisions?

2. Read Acts 24. What words show the effort Tertullus made to gain the favor of Felix (vv. 2-8)?

3. What charges did Tertullus bring against Paul (vv. 5-6)?

4. If you had been a lawyer for Paul's defense, how would you counter this kind of prosecution?

5. How did Paul answer the charges against him (vv. 10-21)? (What did Paul admit and what did he deny?)

6. How did Paul's belief in resurrection influence his life (vv. 15-16 and 21)?

7. If you believed that a person who dies simply ceases to exist in both body and soul, how would you conduct your life differently?

8. What would it mean for you to keep your "conscience clear before God"?

9. What can you know of Felix's attitude toward the Christian faith by the way he handled Paul's legal case (vv. 22-27)?

10. Verse 25 says that Felix was afraid. Why?

11. What part does fear play in your own faith or lack of faith in Jesus?

12. Paul was in the custody of Felix for two years. What opportunities did Felix have during that time?

13. What did you consider in making your own response to the Christian faith? (Or, what do you need to consider before you respond to Jesus?)

14. What is dangerous about saying "Wait" to God?

12
Philemon: Bridging Barriers to Brotherhood

Philemon

During my several decades of Christian faith, I have held (and sometimes overcome) a variety of barriers to close fellowship with other believers. As a high-school student, I favored people of my own church denomination, indeed those within a small fragment of that denomination. During college years, my social conscience kicked in, and I became convinced that wealthy people were almost subhuman, and certainly sub-Christian. At another time (a health awareness era), I found myself disdaining people who were over-weight. And then there was a stage when "kooks" really bugged me. I wanted *my* associates to think straight.

I have almost laughed at myself (and at God), as I have seen him deal with these prejudices of mine. It is as if the minute I have maneuvered myself into one of them, God puts his hand into his many-faceted bag of believers, and pulls out one who illustrates exactly my current favorite prejudice. Then God lays his hand on that person's shoulder and says to me, "This is my child. I love this person. Notice all of his/her wonderful qualities? See, I am showing them to you. You can love this person too."

And the barriers have begun to fall.

---

1. God brings all sorts of people into the Christian faith. What kinds of barriers keep them from feeling like brothers and sisters to each other?

2. In a society where slavery was an established institution that Christians had no authority to change, Paul wrote of how to behave within that framework. Read the book of Philemon. If you were Philemon, would you want to receive this letter from Paul? Explain.

3. Study the greeting of Paul's letter in verses 1-3. What can you know about the writer, the receivers, and the relationship between them?

4. How do Philemon's faith and love form a basis for what Paul is about to ask him to do (vv. 4-7)?

5. What all can you know about Onesimus from verses 8-21?

6. In what different ways does Paul express his love for Onesimus throughout the letter?

How does he express his love for Philemon?

7. When have you particularly enjoyed the love and acceptance of God's people?

8. The name Onesimus means "useful." Yet Paul admits in verse 11 that Onesimus had been useless to Philemon in the past. What steps does Paul take to convince Philemon that Onesimus will now live up to his name (vv. 11-15)?

9. What gentle pressure does Paul exert to ensure that Philemon treats Onesimus as he has requested?

10. If you had been Onesimus, how would you feel returning some one thousand miles to Philemon—with this letter and under these circumstances? (What would you fear? What would you hope for? What temptations would you face?)

11. The Christians mentioned in this letter had to cross many social, economic and geographic barriers in order to relate to each other. When have you benefited from a relationship with a Christian who is vastly different from yourself?

12. How could Paul's instructions in today's study help you rethink your relationship with Christians who don't easily fit into your natural circle of friends?

13. Think of a Christian you know who is on the other side of some potential barrier to your accepting each other as a "dear brother or sister." What can you do to begin to bridge that barrier?

Leader's Notes

Leading a Bible discussion can be an enjoyable and rewarding experience. But it can also be *scary*—especially if you've never done it before. If this is your feeling, you're in good company. When God asked Moses to lead the Israelites out of Egypt, he replied, "O Lord, please send someone else to do it!" (Ex 4:13).

When Solomon became king of Israel, he felt the task was beyond his abilities. "I am only a little child and do not know how to carry out my duties. . . . Who is able to govern this great people of yours?" (1 Kings 3:7, 9).

When God called Jeremiah to be a prophet, he replied, "Ah, Sovereign LORD, . . . I do not know how to speak; I am only a child" (Jer 1:6).

The list goes on. The apostles were "unschooled, ordinary men" (Acts 4:13). Timothy was young, frail and frightened. Paul's "thorn in the flesh" made him feel weak. But God's response to all of his servants—including you—is essentially the same: "My grace is sufficient for you" (2 Cor 12:9). Relax. God helped these people in spite of their weaknesses, and he can help you in spite of your feelings of inadequacy.

There is another reason why you should feel encouraged. Leading a Bible discussion is not difficult if you follow certain guidelines. You don't need to be an expert on the Bible or a trained teacher. The suggestions listed below should enable you to effectively and enjoyably fulfill your role as leader.

Preparing to Lead

1. Ask God to help you understand and apply the passage to your own life. Unless this happens, you will not be prepared to lead others. Pray too for the various members of the group. Ask God to give you an enjoyable and profitable time together studying his Word.

2. As you begin each study, read and reread the assigned Bible passage to familiarize yourself with what the author is saying. In the case of book studies, you may want to read through the entire book prior to the first study. This will give you a helpful overview of its contents.

3. This study guide is based on the New International Version of the Bible. It will help you and the group if you use this translation as the basis for your study and discussion. Encourage others to use the NIV also, but allow them the freedom to use whatever translation they prefer.

4. Carefully work through each question in the study. Spend time in meditation and reflection as you formulate your answers.

5. Write your answers in the space provided in the study guide. This will help you to express your understanding of the passage clearly.

6. It might help you to have a Bible dictionary handy. Use it to look up any unfamiliar words, names or places. (For additional help on how to study a passage, see chapter five of *Leading Bible Discussions*, SU.)

7. Once you have finished your own study of the passage, familiarize yourself with the leader's notes for the study you are leading. These are designed to help you in several ways. First, they tell you the purpose the study guide author had in mind while writing the study. Take time to think through how the study questions work together to accomplish that purpose. Second, the notes provide you with additional background information or comments on some of the questions. This information can be useful if people have difficulty understanding or answering a question. Third, the leader's notes can alert you to potential problems you may encounter during the study.

8. If you wish to remind yourself of anything mentioned in the leader's notes, make a note to yourself below that question in the study.

Leading the Study

1. Begin the study on time. Unless you are leading an evangelistic Bible study, open with prayer, asking God to help you to understand and apply the passage.

2. Be sure that everyone in your group has a study guide. Encourage them to prepare beforehand for each discussion by working through the questions in the guide.

3. At the beginning of your first time together, explain that these studies are meant to be discussions not lectures. Encourage the members of the group to participate. However, do not put pressure on those who may be hesitant to speak during the first few sessions.

4. Read the introductory paragraph at the beginning of the discussion. This will orient the group to the passage being studied.

5. Read the passage aloud if you are studying one chapter or less. You may choose to do this yourself, or someone else may read if he or she has been asked to do so prior to the study. Longer passages may occasionally be read in parts at different times during the study. Some studies may cover several chapters. In such cases reading aloud would probably take too much time, so the group members should simply read the assigned passages prior to the study.

6. As you begin to ask the questions in the guide, keep several things in mind. First, the questions are designed to be used just as they are written. If you wish, you may simply read them aloud to the group. Or you may prefer to express them in your own words. However, unnecessary rewording of the questions is not recommended.

Second, the questions are intended to guide the group toward understanding and applying the *main idea* of the passage. The author of the guide has stated his or her view of this central idea in the *purpose* of the study in the leader's notes. You should try to understand how the passage expresses this idea and how the study questions work together to lead the group in that direction.

There may be times when it is appropriate to deviate from the study guide. For example, a question may have already been answered. If so, move on to the next question. Or someone may raise an important question not covered in the guide. Take time to discuss it! The important thing is to use discretion. There may be many routes you can travel to reach the goal of the study. But the easiest route is usually the one the author has suggested.

7. Avoid answering your own questions. If necessary, repeat or rephrase them until they are clearly understood. An eager group quickly becomes passive and silent if they think the leader will do most of the talking.

8. Don't be afraid of silence. People may need time to think about the question before formulating their answers.

9. Don't be content with just one answer. Ask, "What do the rest of you think?" or "Anything else?" until several people have given answers to the question.

10. Acknowledge all contributions. Try to be affirming whenever possible. Never reject an answer. If it is clearly wrong, ask, "Which verse led you to that conclusion?" or again, "What do the rest of you think?"

11. Don't expect every answer to be addressed to you, even though this will probably happen at first. As group members become more at ease, they will begin to truly interact with each other. This is one sign of a healthy discussion.

12. Don't be afraid of controversy. It can be very stimulating. If you don't resolve an issue completely, don't be frustrated. Move on and keep it in mind for later. A subsequent study may solve the problem.

13. Stick to the passage under consideration. It should be the source for answering the questions. Discourage the group from unnecessary cross-referencing. Likewise, stick to the subject and avoid going off on tangents.

14. Periodically summarize what the *group* has said about the passage. This helps to draw together the various ideas mentioned and gives continuity to the study. But don't preach.

15. Conclude your time together with conversational prayer. Be sure to ask God's help to apply those things which you learned in the study.

16. End on time.

Many more suggestions and helps are found in *Leading Bible Discussions* (SU). Reading and studying through that would be well worth your time.

Components of Small Groups

A healthy small group should do more than study the Bible. There are four components you should consider as you structure your time together.

Nurture. Being a part of a small group should be a nurturing and edifying experience. You should grow in your knowledge and love of God and each other. If we are to properly love God, we must know and keep his commandments (Jn 14:15). That is why Bible study should be a foundational part of your small group. But you can be nurtured by other things as well. You can memorize Scripture, read and discuss a book, or occasionally listen to a tape of a good speaker.

Community. Most people have a need for close friendships. Your small group can be an excellent place to cultivate such relationships. Allow time for informal interaction before and after the study. Have a time of sharing during the meeting. Do fun things together as a group, such as a potluck supper or a picnic. Have someone bring refreshments to the meeting. Be creative!

Worship. A portion of your time together can be spent in worship and prayer. Praise God together for who he is. Thank him for what he has done and is doing in your lives and in the world. Pray for each other's needs. Ask God to help you to apply what you have learned. Sing hymns together.

Mission. Many small groups decide to work together in some form of outreach. This can be a practical way of applying what you have learned. You can host a series of evangelistic discussions for your friends or neighbors. You can visit people at a home for the elderly. Help a widow with cleaning or repair jobs around her home. Such projects can have a transforming influence on your group.

For a detailed discussion of the nature and function of small groups, read *Small Group Leaders' Handbook* or *Good Things Come in Small Groups* (both from SU).

Study 1. Joseph: Parenting in Tough Times. Matthew 1:18-25; 2:13-23.
Purpose: To appreciate the work of a father, as exemplified in Joseph, and to reflect on the impact our families have had on us.

Question 1. Every study begins with an "approach" question, which is meant to be asked before the passage is read. These questions are important for several reasons.

First, they help the group to warm up to each other. No matter how well a group may know each other, there is always a stiffness that needs to be overcome before people will begin to talk openly. A good question will break the ice.

Second, approach questions get people thinking along the lines of the topic of the study. Most people will have lots of different things going on in their minds (dinner, an important meeting coming up, how to get the car fixed) that will have nothing to do with the study. A creative question will get their attention and draw them into the discussion.

Third, approach questions can reveal where our thoughts or feelings need to be transformed by Scripture. That is why it is especially important not to read the passage before the approach question is asked. The passage will tend to color the honest reactions people would otherwise give because they are, of course, supposed to think the way the Bible does. Giving honest responses before they find out what the Bible says may help them see where their thoughts or attitudes need to be changed.

Encourage each person to respond to this question in some way.

Question 2. Find answers throughout the passage. They should include Mary's pregnancy, the angel's announcement, the prophecy, and the absence of sexual union.

Question 3. Let your group be creative. Any number of actions must have come to Joseph's mind—most of them easier (for him) than the one he chose. For his legal rights, see Deuteronomy 22:23-29. In view of these Hebrew religious laws, Joseph was not only extraordinarily kind to Mary; he saved her life!

Question 5. Jesus is Greek for Joshua, which means "the LORD saves." The meaning of Immanuel is explained in the text. Help your group note the meanings of these names as well as the far-reaching implications of their meanings.

Question 7. Use this question to survey all of this text.

Question 8. Let several people speculate about what might have gone through Joseph's mind during the various decisions he had to make throughout this period. For an imaginative picture of what might have occurred during the flight into Egypt see Madeleine L'Engle's *Dance in the Desert* (New York: Farrar, Straus & Giroux, 1969).

Questions 10-11. Use these questions to refer to either a family of origin (birth family) or a present family, if two families exist. Be alert to the possibility that some in the group may have experienced serious family disorder so that they rarely felt protected at home. They may have even experienced abuse. Handle this potential situation as gently as possible. Then proceed to the next question. God can use even dysfunctional families to show our need for him and for other believers. He can build on that hurt to nurture spiritual growth.

Study 2. Anna and Simeon: Growing Old with God. Luke 2:21-40.

Purpose: To see Anna and Simeon as examples of how we can grow in service of God as grow older.

Question 1. Try to involve each person with this question. If some members of the group already consider themselves "old" ask, "What do you want to be like when you are old*er?"*

Question 2. Study verses 21-24. Your group should find that Christ's parents took him to Jerusalem to be circumcised, to be consecrated to the Lord, and to offer a sacrifice. For the legal basis of these practices, see Leviticus 12:2-3 regarding circumcision. See Numbers 3:11-13 regarding consecration of the firstborn, and Leviticus 5:11 regarding the offering. (Use these references for your own background information. There is no need to take the group to them unless questions of background arise.)

Question 3. Your group should notice that Simeon was "wise," "devout," "waiting," "the Holy Spirit was upon him," "God had revealed certain things about the future to him," God's Spirit had sent him to the temple courts, and he was ready to praise God. Once your group has noted this information in the text, help them to discuss the kind of character that Simeon had developed that would allow him to make these preparations, and that would allow God to use him in that way.

Question 4. Discuss the meaning of Simeon's various pronouncements. If you need a follow-up question ask, "Examine each of Simeon's statements. What does it reveal of God's plan?"

Question 5. Compare verse 26 with the content of Simeon's prayer.

Question 6. Encourage each person to express the longings and hopes that could lead them to this satisfying conclusion at the end of life. Help people to be as specific and personal as their trust of each other will allow.

Question 7. Use the information in verses 36-37.

Question 8. Notice verse 38 as it relates to Anna's history of worship in verses 36-37.

Question 9. Compare the description of Christ in verses 39-40 with the mission that Anna and Simeon had just revealed.

Questions 10-11. Allow time to discuss these questions in personal and specific ways.

Study 3. A Throw-away Woman: Redeemed by Christ. John 8:1-11.
Purpose: To value all people, because Christ values them.

Question 1. For an optional follow-up question ask, "When have you seen someone treated as if he or she were disposable?"

Question 2. According to verse 1, while other people went home, Jesus went to the Mount of Olives, where he may have spent the night in prayer. Verse 2 finds Jesus already in the temple courts at dawn, where a crowd gathered around his teaching. There, he was a handy target for religious leaders, who probably felt that he had invaded their territory.

Note on authenticity of the text: John 7:53—8:11 does not appear in the most ancient texts. At question, however, is not whether the event occurred, but where it fits in the biblical account. Merrill C. Tenney comments as follows: "To say that the passage is not an integral part of JOHN does not dismiss it, however. It is still necessary to account for its presence. Even those who exclude it from the body of JOHN on textual grounds admit that its tenor is wholly in keeping with the character and ministry of Jesus, and that it doubtless constitutes a genuine account of an episode of His career, though it may by misplaced" (*John: The Gospel of Belief* [Grand Rapids, Mich.: Eerdmans, 1948], p. 138).

Question 3. Your group should cite several phrases from the text: "brought in a woman," "They made her stand," "this woman" (no name), "They were using . . ."

Question 4. Encourage several personal accounts. Be sure to address both sections of the question.

Question 5. A variety of reasons might explain the behavior of these religious leaders. Had they set a trap for the woman, as well as Jesus, with a promise to let her partner go free? Did they value her less than the man because she was a woman? Was her partner actually one of the accusers? Did she commit adultery so frequently that it was easy to catch her? Let your group pose several possible explanations.

Question 6. These clever leaders were trying to catch Jesus between two sets of laws. The Hebrew religious law of Leviticus demanded the death penalty. Yet Roman political law denied enforcement. If Jesus permitted the stoning, he could be tried in Roman courts for murder. If he refused to permit it, he could be tried in Jewish courts for heresy—and publicly discredited as a religious teacher.

If your group wants additional background information ask, "What protection did Hebrew law grant against executing an innocent person?" (See Deut 17:2-7.)

Question 7. By this time your group should see that this whole incident was a smoke screen for many larger issues: Christ's authority, the authority of Jewish law, the value of the woman's life, the comparative value of her partner's life, and the nature of sin—the woman's *and* her accuser's.

Question 8. If you need a follow-up question ask, "Did Jesus excuse the woman's actions? Explain."

Question 9. Compare verses 7 and 11.

Question 11. If you want an additional question that points back to the text at this point ask, "What lasting effects do you think this event had on the woman?"

Study 4. A Blind Beggar: Seeing Jesus with Open Eyes. John 9.

Purpose: To appreciate Christ's work in our lives as it leads us to faith in him.

Question 1. Some people may remember Jesus from early childhood. They may recall a Sunday-school picture, an art piece, a story told by a parent, a song ("Jesus Loves Me"), a feeling or impression of what Jesus is like. Those who learned of Jesus in later years will have more clear memories of their first impressions. Help people to describe these mental pictures, then to discuss their reactions to those impressions: positive? negative? accurate? mistaken? This question should form a backdrop for later discussion of the way their faith in Jesus developed through various stages.

Question 3. The blind man might have felt reassured by Christ's statement that neither he nor his parents had sinned and thereby caused his blindness. (What an awful burden of accusation to carry through life!) He might have felt overwhelmed or confused that somehow God's work would be displayed in his life. As for Christ's references to day and night and light, we can only guess what these would have meant to a man blind from birth.

Question 4. Notice that the beggar submitted to Christ's "treatment" which must have seemed a bit odd, not to mention humiliating. And he went willingly to wash in the pool of Siloam—some distance away. In fact, he wasn't healed until he had actually left Jesus and gone to the pool. Help your group to study the beggar's words as he attempted to explain what had happened to him. The words coupled with his actions will help describe his faith.

Question 6. These references to sin are hardly more than slurs against a person's birth. In verses 1-2, even the disciples seemed to assume that the beggar's blindness was a result of sin, perhaps a sin his parents had committed. They suspected that God had punished them by taking out his anger on their infant. In verse 29 the Pharisees slandered Christ's origins. (Were they still wondering about who Christ's father was? Did Mary and Joseph suffer raised eyebrows because of Christ's birth so few months after their marriage? Was Jesus sometimes called a bastard? It seems so here.) Verse 34 points again to the beggar's birth. The question here is not so much one of "original sin," which everyone holds in common, but of this particular birth being sinful. Let your group discuss the pain of these kinds of accusations. Then discuss the view of sin that they assume.

As for what is wrong with this view of sin, Christ responded in part to that question in verse 3. God had chosen to glorify himself through the suffering of the beggar and through the suffering of his parents. Sin was not the cause of their hurt. The blind man's accusers were making the same mistake that we often hear today; we may even accuse ourselves in the same way. We wonder, "Am I sick because I sinned? Did someone I love die because I sinned, or because he or she sinned? Or, conversely, am I healthy and wealthy because I am doing what pleases God?"

"No" is the answer to all of these accusations! God is not a puppet whose kindness or anger we can flick on and off by our offerings of good and bad deeds. His purposes are beyond our comprehension. Sometimes he matures us through suffering. Sometimes he draws us to experience him more deeply because of our pain. Sometimes he enters our lives, quite without our prompting, and brings glory to himself.

The accusation of the Pharisees in verse 34 raises another false view of sin. Even if the beggar's birth had been a birth that grew out of sin, did that mean that he could not experience right relationship with God? Certainly not. God chose the beggar as an instrument through which to glorify himself. If the Pharisees had been willing to listen to him, they too could have received the forgiving grace of Jesus.

Question 7. Compare the conversation between the Pharisees in verse 16 with the beggar's reasoning in verses 17 and 30-32.

If you want an additional question here, ask: "The beggar believed in Jesus at this point, at least in part, because of what Jesus had done for him. What has God done in your own life that has helped you to believe in him?"

Question 8. When the Pharisees "threw him out" of the temple, the healed beggar was excommunicated from public worship—a serious penalty then as now. It was because of this threat that his parents had refused to testify at all (v. 22). Yet the blind man, even in the early stages of faith, and even before he knew much about Jesus, took this risk—and suffered its loss. Let your group discuss how this prepared him for the next conversation with Jesus—and a more thorough knowledge of him and commitment to him.

Question 9. Discuss each statement of faith separately. Of each one, ask: "What does the beggar believe about Jesus at this point?" If you have discussed aspects of this question at previous steps, just review what you concluded and go on.

Question 10. Use this question to help people reflect on stages of their own spiritual growth.

Question 12. Pace your study so that you leave enough time for thoughtful responses to this question about the darker stages of our lives. Be comforted that God glorified himself through the beggar's blindness. He also allowed the beggar to know Jesus as a result. God may use your own dark times for similar good purpose.

As your group discusses this question, encourage conversation to move from past to present and then to future tense. Ask, "How might your current experiences of dark times deepen your faith in Jesus? How can you begin to prepare for future times of darkness so that they do not devastate your faith?"

Study 5. Lazarus: A Man Who Died Twice. John 11:1-44.

Purpose: To improve our ability to give comfort because of Christ's power over death.

Question 2. The text gives several clues to the relationship. Mary, Martha and Lazarus were siblings (v. 1). Mary served and worshiped Jesus, mentioned here in verse 2 but actually occurring at a later time as recorded in John 12:1-3. Jesus loved this family (vv. 3 and 5).

Question 3. Let your group notice the concerns of the disciples mentioned in verses 8, 12 and 16. Then discuss the probable worries and conversations on this full day of walking.

Question 4. Study each of Christ's comments: verses 4, 9-10, 11 and 14. The disciples may not have understood all that Jesus said, but with hindsight, your group may be able to interpret much of it.

Regarding Christ's comments about day and light in verse 9, Jesus was addressing their fears about his personal safety so near Jerusalem. In essence, he was saying, "My life will have enough time for me to do what needs to be done, no more and no less." (A look ahead at the end of this chapter and the events following shows that the fears of the disciples were well-founded.)

Question 7. Study each phrase of Christ's strong statement in verse 25. Help your group discuss the measure of comfort each would bring. If you want additional questions at this point, ask: "Jesus ended his explanation to Martha with the words, 'Do you believe this?' How would you answer that question? Explain." You may also add, "How might Christ's words here speak to your own fears of death?"

Question 9. Jesus *talked* with Martha. But with Mary, who appeared more distraught at the moment, his *actions* spoke comfort. He accompanied Mary to the grave and wept there with her.

Question 10. Three times people voiced objection that Jesus was not present when Lazarus died. Discuss their implied understanding of his power, what they assumed to the be the limits of his power, and also Christ's own statement in verse 4. If you need a clarifying question, ask: "Verses 5-6 say, 'Jesus loved Martha and her sister and Lazarus. Yet . . . he stayed where he was two more days.' Why?"

Question 11. Use this question to sense the reactions of the crowd during the series of events in verses 38-44. Then discuss potential questions raised by the events.

Question 12. Use this question to help your group think more personally about life, death, and life after death. You may also wish to use follow-up questions, such as, "Would this experience cause you to value life more or less? Explain. How do you think you would approach death the second time?"

Question 13. Also draw on responses from question 6.

Study 6. Mary Magdalene: Loving Jesus in Practical Ways. Luke 8:1-3; Mark 15:37-47; John 20:1-18.

Purpose: To follow Mary Magdalene's example of finding practical ways to express our love for Jesus.

Question 3. Your group may think of a variety of reasons Mary Magdalene was at the cross. (Most of the disciples had gone into hiding.) Suggestions might include because she loved him, because her friends were there, because the disciples had fled and she felt that some of Christ's followers ought to be with him, because she wanted to help with the burial, because she wanted to show Jesus that she still cared.

Question 4. Your group should pick out virtually all of the information in the text. Notice especially the words of the centurion in verse 39, the torn temple veil in verse 38, and the place of his burial in verse 47.

The New International Version Study Bible (Kenneth Barker, gen. ed. [Hodder & Stoughton, 1985]) comments on the temple veil: "The curtain that separated the Holy Place from the Most Holy Place (Ex 26:31-33). The tearing of the curtain indicated that Christ had entered heaven itself for us so that we too may now enter God's very presence (Heb 9:8-10, 12; 10:19-20)" (p. 1529).

Be sure that your group speaks of all four sections of this question. Consider treating what Mary saw and heard first, then what she learned, and finally what she must have felt.

Question 6. Allow time for thoughtful responses here. Not many people today believe that they have been inhabited by demons, but all of us see evil forces upon our lives. Help your group to discuss the evil that has touched their lives, then talk about ways that Christ has helped them to battle that evil.

Question 7. Cite "clues" throughout this passage. If you would like an additional question at this point, ask: "If you could interview the people there, what further questions would you ask?"

Questions 10-11. Christ's resurrection is central to the Christian faith. Eyewitnesses, like Mary Magdalene, verified the event. If group members need further information about the importance of the resurrection, refer them to 1 Corinthians 15 for later reading.

Question 12. Find information in Luke 8:3; Mark 15:40-41, 47; John 20:15, 18.

Study 7. Thomas: Disciple of Doubt. John 14:1-7; 20:19-31.

Purpose: To acknowledge our doubts and to grow, like Thomas, from doubt into deepened faith.

Question 5. Encourage responses from several people. Help them to speak not only of *what* comforts them in these verses, but *how* it comforts them and in what specific situations.

Question 6. Notice the locked door, the fear, Christ's appearance, his declaration of peace, the evidence of wounds in his hands and side, the joy of the disciples, and the various aspects of Christ's commission to them in verses 21-22.

Note on verse 23: What did Jesus mean about forgiving and not forgiving sins? *The NIV Study Bible* comments, "God does not forgive people's sins because we do so, nor does he withhold forgiveness because we do. Rather, those who proclaim the gospel are in effect forgiving or not forgiving sins, depending on whether the hearers accept or reject Jesus Christ" (p. 1637).

Question 7. Study verses 24-25 and discuss the probable differences in attitude, mood, actions, feelings, plans for the future. Discuss also their probable relationships and tensions with each other.

Question 9. Contrast the Thomas your group envisioned in question 7 with the statement of verse 28. Let your group describe the changes in what Thomas believed about Jesus, in what he felt about his fellow disciples, in his emotional state, and in his plans for his future. Your group may make observations similar to those of Merrill C. Tenney in *John: The Gospel of Belief* (Grand Rapids, Mich.: Eerdmans, 1948):

Thomas was a living demonstration of the power of Christ to dispel doubt. He was naturally of a pessimistic temperament as his previous utterances showed (11:16, 14:5), and his doubt seems to have been the product of his pessimism rather than lack of confidence in Jesus Himself. After all, he knew that Jesus had died, and he could say, "The worst has happened just as I said it would." Jesus volunteered to submit to the very test that Thomas had demanded. The fact the He knew what Thomas had said when He was not present was convincing proof of His supernatural knowledge, and His willingness to accept Thomas on his own terms was a marvel of condescension and compassion. It is unthinkable that Thomas did actually put Jesus' body to the test. All his unbelief vanished as he worshipped. For a Jew to salute another man, however he might revere him, as "Lord and God" (28) could only mean that he had come to the point of worshipping Him as deity. The resurrection made the difference between the skepticism of despair and the worship that brings certainty.

Thus belief in a risen Christ made a mourner into a missionary, a penitent into a preacher, the bereaved friend into an apostle of love, a timid and shrinking coterie of disciples into fearless heralds of a new movement, and a doubter into a confessor. With the confession of Thomas, John reached the high peak of belief: faith can rise no higher than when it avows Jesus of Nazareth to be its Lord and God. (p. 284)

Question 10. Your group should notice and comment on particular phrases, "Those who have not seen . . . believed" (v. 29), "that you may believe" (v. 30), "that you may have life" (v. 31). Encourage people to comment on the specific personal significance of these phrases to them as individuals.

If time allows, you may wish to follow this question with a look at the witnesses in John 20:1-18. Consider the gravestone, the grave clothes, Mary Magdalene, Peter, the other disciple, the Ten and Thomas. Discuss how these witnesses address our potential doubts about Jesus.

Questions 11-12. Allow adequate time for several individuals to speak of their personal responses to doubt and renewed faith, as well as to the life created by faith in Jesus.

Study 8. Simon: Bargaining with God. Acts 8:9-25.

Purpose: To worship God for who he is, rather than trying to bargain with God for what he can give us.

Question 2. Your group should notice such words as: "sorcery," "amazed all the people," "boasted that he was someone great," "people both high and low gave him their attention," "divine power," "Great Power," "magic," "believed," "baptized," "astonished." Discuss what these words reveal of Simon's personality and character.

Question 3. Your group should discuss Simon's charismatic character as well as the evil power that he seemed to possess. Notice the character of his followers. The power that they attributed to him bordered on idolatry. Notice also their willingness to follow: first they followed Simon, then they followed Philip—with what appears to be little regard for the opposite spiritual forces at work.

Question 4. Simon could not continue to allow people to follow him in the same way that they had in the past. He could not allow people to think of him as "divine" or "the Great Power." Christ must take that position. In addition, Simon must become aware that his use of sorcery was aligning him with the supernatural evil powers mentioned in the laws of the Old Testament (see Ex 22:18 and Deut 18:9-14), and that he must oppose that power.

Question 5. Study the purpose that Peter and John had in coming to Samaria and also what they accomplished in the trip. Notice particularly how the Samaritans received the Holy Spirit in verse 17. In view of Simon's request in verses 18-19, we can assume that the presence of the Holy Spirit was made known in some obvious way, perhaps with signs similar to those that evidenced his presence in Acts 2.

Question 6. Study verses 18-19. Your group should notice that Simon did not ask for the Holy Spirit. He asked, instead, that he be given the ability to transmit the Holy Spirit—just as he had seen Peter and John do by placing their hands on believers.

Question 7. Simon may have planned any number of uses for that gift. He may have genuinely desired to be an instrument of God's power. But, in view of his history as a sorcerer and magician, we can guess that he wanted to incorporate this divine gift into his magic act. Small wonder that Peter was so incensed at the request.

Question 8. Look beyond what Simon asked, to what his request testified about his view of God. Did he see God as one who would take a bribe? As one who would not give what was good unless he were paid? As one who chose to give gifts, not because of how they would be used, but because of who paid? Did Simon think he could earn God's favor? Ask your group to try to describe the kind of God that Simon envisioned with his request.

If you have time for an extra question at this point, ask: "What is wrong with viewing God and his gifts in this way?"

Question 9. Notice the phrases, "you thought you could buy," "you have no part," "your heart is not right," "wickedness," "thought in your heart," "bitterness," "captive to sin." These words go beyond Simon's request to buy power. They strike at Simon's character and core. The request grew out of a core that was not right with God and that perceived God in a totally wrong way.

Question 10. Opinions about the extent of Simon's repentance will vary. But his statement seems relatively mild and self-serving when compared to the accusation Peter had just made.

Was Simon a true believer? *The NIV Study Bible* comments, "It is difficult to know whether Simon's faith was genuine. Even though Luke says Simon believed, Peter's statement that Simon had no part in the apostles' ministry because his heart was not 'right before God' (v. 21) casts some doubt" (pp. 1658-59).

Question 11. People try to use a variety of "bargaining chips" with God, bargaining chips like prayer, self-denial, money, good deeds. Even though these all have a valued place in the life of believers, your group should discuss appropriate and inappropriate uses. Motives will be a major clue. Do we primarily want to win God's favor—and gifts? Or do we want to please him out of love and thanksgiving and thereby serve his people?

Question 12. If time allows, you may wish to precede this question with the following question: "Take stock of your usual habits of prayer. What percent of your praying would you guess is devoted to asking God to do or give something?"

Study 9. A Prison Guard: Getting Free from Internal Prisons. Acts 16:6-40.

Purpose: To give and receive nurture from our church as we participate together in the freedom of Christ's redemption.

Question 1. Use these questions to help members of the group orient themselves to each other's general church ties. Gain insight into what is valuable and what is missing in each other's relationships with churches. If members of your group do not attend church, ask, "What would you want to see in a church?"

Question 2. Study first the route Paul took in verses 6-10. (Use a map.) Notice the various ways God led him to Philippi. Notice also the pronoun "we" in verse 10, an indication that Luke, the writer of Acts, has joined Paul's party. (This is his first appearance in Acts.) After you have studied this paragraph, move on to verses 11-15 to discuss the initial steps in forming the church once Paul arrived in Philippi.

Question 3. Your group should have a variety of observations based on Lydia's character as she appears in the text. Samples include: she attended a prayer group and therefore already valued worship with a cluster of people, she was a business woman, she already worshiped the true God, she responded readily to the gospel of Jesus, she was able to influence her household in matters of faith, she chose to be baptized immediately, she demanded that Paul recognize her faith ("If you consider me a believer . . ."), she was hospitable, and she was able to "persuade" Paul—no small task.

Question 4. Answers to this question are not readily apparent in the text. If the group seems confused, a preliminary question may help: "Who all used the slave girl—and for what purposes?" Here your group may begin to discover that even though the girl was giving correct information about God, that knowledge would not likely be accepted because of her condition. In fact, she might unintentionally bring embarrassment to the church. In addition, her owners were using her for their own profit—as was Satan himself as he tried to embarrass and annoy Paul and his followers.

It is interesting to notice that later, when the frightened jailer asked for Paul's help, he, like the demented slave girl, spoke of being "saved." (Compare verse 17 with verse 30.) The power of Jesus Christ eventually freed them both.

Question 5. Not many people today feel that they have had contact with evil spirits. But evil comes in a variety of forms. Help your group to name some of the evil influences that they must cope with and how that evil threatens them.

Question 7. Use the information in verses 19-21 as well as the background information in the chapter introduction. A fledgling church hardly needs a major ethnic and religious controversy with the local government—then or now.

Question 8. Regarding the jailer's circumstances, it is interesting to read Acts 12:18-19, which shows something of the pressure he would have been under.

Look at all that God did through natural forces, Paul and Silas, and the jailer's own bosses. Notice the joyful faith that Paul and Silas displayed in verse 25, in spite of their condition and the treatment they had received. Notice the timely earthquake and the way it affected his jail. Notice that not only did Paul and Silas stay in the opened jail—but so did the other prisoners. (Were they, too, influenced by the faith of Paul and Silas?) Notice that Paul stopped the jailer's attempted suicide just in time. Study Paul's explanation of the gospel in verses 31-32. Then notice the second miracle in the jailer's life. He would not have to re-imprison Paul and Silas—or answer for their absence in jail. In the morning, the magistrates sent new orders that they be released (vv. 35-36). These were not simply the actions of people and nature. They were God at work, taking action to free the jailer from his own inner prison.

Questions 9-10. Help your group to discuss these two aspects of Christ as Lord: the freedom and the structure. Jesus is, after all, our Lord. While he grants us freedom from guilt and punishment for sin and freedom from the power of evil, he also brings us under a new authority—his own. Help your group to discuss specific examples of these in their own lives.

Question 11. Study the jailer's character as it is revealed throughout the text. Look particularly at verses 29-34.

Question 12. Paul claimed his rights as a Roman citizen, a strong defense against the charge brought in verse 21. And he insisted on leaving the city with the greatest dignity and only after bidding a proper farewell to the church. Discuss ways that this would continue to benefit the church as it remained in the community.

Question 13. Paul exhibited great protectiveness toward the church he had helped to found. Help group members to discuss concerns about their own churches and how they can best contribute to their continued well-being.

Study 10. Priscilla and Aquila: Practicing Hospitality. Acts 18.

Purpose: To follow the example of Priscilla and Aquila as we use our homes to extend biblical hospitality.

Question 1. Be aware that not everyone in your group may have a "home" from which to practice hospitality. Structure the discussion so that it can also include those who live in apartments, rented rooms, dormitories, etc. Our homes do not have to be spacious in order for us to practice hospitality. (Abraham practiced hospitality from a tent! See Genesis 4.) Even those who live in rooms or apartments will have a favorite lunch counter, a favorite view, a neighborhood recreation room. Some of the best memories are created from a blanket roll on the sofa, or a "picnic" on the floor. And hospitality need not involve overnight guests.

Then discuss favorite symbols of hospitality from the perspective of guest:

clean sheets, a hug at the door, an unharried host or hostess, being able to participate in the family routine. Expect different preferences from different people. You may discover that some of your own frantic preparations are not significant to many guests.

Question 2. Survey the passages. See especially Acts 18:2-3, 26, as well as Romans 16:3-5.

Question 3. Study the details of Paul's stay in Corinth (Acts 18:1-17). His stay was long (more than a year and a half). Paul was stubborn, abrasive, a constant source of controversy, with many enemies. Examine the text for examples of what it must have been like to have Paul as a houseguest.

Questions 6-7. Discuss the mutual benefit of this long stay together. Use a little sanctified imagination as you discuss their practical and spiritual contributions to each other. Be sure that any speculations do not disagree with the text.

Paul taught about Jesus on three missionary journeys spread over about twenty years. Yet his longest visits were centered around Corinth and Ephesus. On his second trip, Paul spent nearly two years in Corinth, a Greek cultural and religious center. (Corinth was also known as a sexual playground.) On his third trip, Paul spent nearly three years in Ephesus, a Turkish port city just two hundred miles across the Aegean Sea from Corinth. While these trips become well-defined on a map, the biblical text almost merges them as one. Acts 18:22 ends the second trip and Acts 18:23 begins the third. Meanwhile, Priscilla and Aquila, who hosted Paul's center of ministry in Corinth on the second trip, form a connecting link as they awaited his arrival in Ephesus.

Question 9. See Acts 18:20, 26 and 27. From these examples we see that hospitality among first-century Christians was common. In fact, Paul probably stayed with other believers throughout his route.

Question 11. For Apollos, Priscilla and Aquila went beyond mere bed and breakfast service. They noticed the educational and spiritual gaps in Apollos— and tutored him. (Living and traveling with the apostle Paul gave them more than adequate teaching credentials.) Then they arranged further hospitality for him as Apollos took up his own missionary work.

Question 12. Discuss the practical work involved, the preparation, the cleaning, the lack of privacy, the clutter. Then discuss the potential rewards of this work—both for the host and for the church.

Question 13. Encourage practical and personal responses to this question. Hosting a church is a task beyond most of our abilities or opportunities. But we can serve God through hospitality in a variety of ways. Let your group explore some creative ideas. For example: caring for a neighbor's child, foster parenting, letting your family kitchen become a drop-in center for your teenager's friends, hosting a Bible study or prayer group, using your kitchen to prepare a meal for someone who is ill, using your phone to listen to people who need an understanding ear, making phone calls to people who are housebound, inviting a new person in your neighborhood for dessert and coffee—and encouraging a conversation that would make it easy to mention God's work in your life, tutoring a child who has difficulty in school, making a home where your own children feel warm and welcome, creating an atmosphere where mention of God's kindness is a natural part of conversation. Gauge your time so that each person in your group is able to mention some way of using his or her home to accomplish God's work.

Study 11. Governor Felix: Saying "Wait" to God. Acts 24.

Purpose: To reexamine the invitation to faith in Jesus and our response to that invitation.

Question 5. Your group should mention a dozen or more of the details in verses 10-21.

Question 6. Discuss the ways that Paul allowed his belief in resurrection to influence his life. If you want an additional question at this point, ask: "Why might belief in resurrection be a source of both dread and hope?" Be sure that your group notices Paul's belief that both the righteous and the wicked will return to life (v. 15). From other passages (Jn 5:28-29; Rev 20:12-15), we know that judgement will ensue.

Question 9. Study Felix's words and actions in verses 22-27. Your group should notice that Felix was both attracted and repulsed by what Paul had to say—and that he was also afraid.

Question 10. Notice what Paul was speaking of when Felix became afraid: righteousness, self-control, judgment. Discuss how Felix would likely feel about these qualities in view of his actions and personality as described in the introductory paragraph.

Question 12. Felix had as much opportunity to hear from Paul as did Priscilla and Aquila. Indeed, Paul spent more time in the company of this Roman ruler than he did in founding any single church, with the exception of the church at Ephesus.

Felix could have set Paul free. He could have executed Paul. Or he could have been converted. Discuss Felix's opportunity, what he won and what he lost.

Question 13. Create an atmosphere that allows honesty from those who have already come to faith in Jesus as well as for those who have not yet taken this step. Treat doubts and questions with respect.

Study 12. Philemon: Bridging Barriers to Brotherhood. Philemon.

Purpose: To use the instructions for Christian love between Onesimus and Philemon as an inspiration to bridge our own barriers between believers.

Question 1. Encourage your group to mention a variety of barriers: social, psychological, economic, geographic, racial and others. If people can cite specific examples of these barriers, as they have seen or experienced them, you will have a head start on later discussion.

Question 4. Faith and love form a solid basis for Paul's request. Philemon loved God, and he loved Paul. Because Paul and God also loved Onesimus, Philemon might be expected to allow Onesimus to join that circle. In addition, Philemon's faith is a basis for action. Philemon became a Christian the way that everyone else does: not through any merit of his own, but through the generosity of Jesus Christ (Eph 2:8-10). He could not, therefore, expect Onesimus to earn his way to Christ—or to himself. In God's sight, Philemon and Onesimus were equals: unworthy, but redeemed.

Question 6. Paul's love drenches this letter. Find as many illustrations of that love as you can—love for Onesimus and love for Philemon. It is his love (and God's) for both that allows Paul to make his request.

Question 7. Wait for several people to respond. Ask questions that will help them to be as specific and personal as is appropriate.

Question 9. See verses 8-9, 17-21, and 22.

Question 10. Paul says several times that he is a prisoner. We may therefore expect that he wrote this letter from Rome during his imprisonment there. In that case, Onesimus was traveling (perhaps alone) nearly a thousand miles on foot and by boat to his owner in Colosse. He would have had lots of time to worry and think, numerous opportunities to turn back, or to go elsewhere—and numerous reasons to do so. Let your group try to think and feel his emotions.

It is also possible that Onesimus's trip was shorter. Some scholars believe that Paul may have written this letter from Ephesus, that his "imprisonment" was his way of describing his bondage to Jesus Christ. In that case, Onesimus's trip was considerably shorter—a mere two hundred miles.

Questions 11-13. Pace your study so that you have adequate time to discuss these questions. Encourage each person to respond in some way.

Carolyn Nystrom is an editor of adult education at Victor Books. She has written over 55 children's books and Bible study guides, including six Christian Character Bible Studies and the LifeBuilders 1 & 2 Peter and Jude and Old Testament Kings. She and her husband, Roger, live in St. Charles, Illinois, with an assortment of cats and kids and quilts.